AWESOME WORDS
FOR GEEKS & NERDS

A Funny Guide For Word-Savvy Kids ...And Word-Challenged Adults

Words by **Rocket Roddy**
Pictures by **Rocket Roddy & Missy Elettra**

For **"Miss Thelma"**
Nurturer, Role Model, Supporter
The Ultimate Trifecta For A Loving Son
Thanks Mom!

Copyright © 2021 by Rocket Roddy

All rights reserved. No part of this book may be reproduced, distributed, or transmitted in any form or by any means, including photocopying, recording, or other electronic or mechanical methods, without the prior written permission of the publisher, except in the case of brief quotations embodied in critical reviews and certain other noncommercial uses permitted by copyright law.

www.RocketRoddyAuthor.com

ISBN: 978-0-929458-00-7 (Hardcover)
978-0-929458-01-4 (Softcover)
978-0-929458-03-8 (Ebook)

Five Things To Know About This Book

Hi – this is Rocket Roddy with helpful news for YOU.

1 Would you like a FREE, coloring-book version of AWESOME WORDS FOR GEEKS & NERDS? It's an abridged, 12-page, PDF file. (The regular coloring book is 40-pages.) If you're interested, go to Rocket Roddy's website –www.RocketRoddyAuthor.com– and ask for the "FREE, coloring-book PDF file."

2 Who is "Mimi"? At the lower right corner of each illustration in this book you'll see the word "Mimi" followed by a number. "Mimi" is my Wonder Dog. The number following her name on the lower-right corner of each illustration alerts you to how many times I have hidden Mimi's name in that particular illustration. There are a total of 112 "hidden Mimis" in this book. I'm wondering – will you be able to find ALL of them?

3 Do YOU have a favorite "Awesome Nerd Word" that you'd like to see in the next version of this book? If so, please send it to me. If I include it in the next volume of AWFG&N, YOU will receive (a) TWO, autographed copies of book #2, (b) AND I'll make special mention of your name on the "acknowledgements" page.

4 Would you like to HEAR the audio-version of this book, read by Rocket Roddy? (Between you and me, this makes the book an even better, and funnier, experience.) Again, just visit my website – www.RocketRoddyAuthor.com

5 Mimi and I would LOVE to know your opinion about this book. If you enjoy it, please give it 5 "stars" on Amazon or elsewhere. Better yet, please add a sentence or two as to what you liked best about it. Or, if you aren't so keen about the book, that also could be valuable news to other would-be buyers. In that case, give it just 4 (or 3 – ouch) stars. But again, please share with Mimi and me why you felt that way. (Did you want different words, or different pictures? Is there a change you'd like to see in the next version of this book?) Whatever your feelings about this book, YOUR opinion matters. Other would-be readers will VALUE your input.

Mimi just barked her own approval. "Atta girl, Mimi!"

If An Elephant Is **Effusive**, What Does That Mean?

An elephant who's **effusive**, is gushingly unchic.
She trumpets out her pleasure, while kissing both your cheeks.

Effusive (eh-FYOO siv) *Noun* — An expression of excessive emotions; fulsome; overdone; expressing feelings of gratitude or pleasure in a gushing or unrestrained manner.

If her Highness sends an invite to share a spot of tea,
Miss Packy squeals effusively: "Ooooh, Queenie, tea 'n me!"

If A Hippo Favors **Hypocorism** – What Does That Mean?

If a hippo calls his best friend "bubba" – and his girlfriend "sweetie-pie."
If "Nana" is the term he calls his mama's mother by,

Hypocorism (Hy-pawk-or-izm) *Noun* – Shorter form of a given name. A pet name or nickname. Usually meant as an endearment. Sometimes silly syllables: "Mooky," "Shnookums," "Booboo," "Sugarpuss."

That's called **hypocorism** – a fancy word, no shame.
Just a hippo's hip, endearing way of bestowing fave pet names.

If Sir Piggy Makes A **Portmanteau**, What Does <u>That</u> Mean?

Sir Piggy likes to take two words: example, "smoke" and "fog,"
Then make a **portmanteau** of them, creating one word, "smog."

Portmanteau (port-MAN-toe) *Noun* — A large suitcase with 2 equal halves; a word whose meaning and form are derived from blending 2 other different words.

Why mix "gigantic" with "enormous"? To make the grander term "ginormous." In short, two words scrunched up just so, Sir Piggy calls a **portmanteau**.

If A Snake's Name Is **Sesquipedalian**, What Does That Mean?

"Wriggling-longissimus," a type snake I hope misses us,"
Is a **sesquipedalian** term.

Sesquipedalian (ses-kwi-peh-DAY-lee-un) *Noun* – Any very long word; from Latin, meaning "foot-and-a-half"; also, long-winded.

You may think it sounds alien, but **sesquipedalian**,
Merely describes any snake–long word.

If A Bullfrog Has **Bupkes**, What Does That Mean?

If a bullfrog has **bupkes**, it means he's got nothing,
'Though the source phrase for **bupkes** is a wee-tad disgusting.

Bupkes (BUP-kiss) *Noun* — Worthless, absolutely nothing, zip, zilch, nada.

This Yiddish phrase means: "small poops from a goat."
So when Froggy thinks **bu-u-u-pkes**, he smiles, then he croaks.

If A Raccoon's a **Rascal**, What Does That Mean?

Raccoons are true **rascals**; they're light-fingered scamps.
So savvy young Scouts keep those thieves from their camps.

Rascal (RAS-kul) *Noun* — A scoundrel; playfully mischievous; a dishonest person

'Cause if one steals your backpack, I pity your task.
You can't I.D. **rascals** if they're all born with masks!

If A Caterpillar's Life Is **Inchoate**, What Does That Mean?

MIMI 6

I drew up half a plan today; it's still too soon to show it.
When things are not yet fully formed, we say they are **inchoate**.

Inchoate (in-KOH-uht) *Noun* — Not completely formed or developed yet; an idea or image just beginning to take shape; something only partially done; lacking shape or organization.

MIMI 3

The same is true for caterpillars, 'though they never know it.
Until reborn as butterflies, they crawl through life, **inchoate**.

17

K

A Kangaroo Kerfuffle – What Does That Mean?

Kerfuffle means a ruckus, a hassle, or a brawl.
A kangaroo **kerfuffle** might mean boxing one and all.

Kerfuffle (ker–FUH–full) *Noun* — Some kind of disturbance, scandal, fight, or mess

To save yourself a shiner, this warning is for you,
Make peace with your next kanga, and evade **kerfuffle**-roos.

If You Give An Ant **Affront**, What Does That Mean?

We're jungle ants, yo! We swarm by the millions.
We dine on fresh greens, tho' we're colored vermilion.

Affront (uh-FRUNT) *Noun* – Intentional insult or offense.
Vermilion (ver-MIL-ion) *Noun* – A vivid, reddish-orange.
Grunt (grunt) *Noun* – Acronym for military infantry soldier: General Replacement, UNTrained.

We're professional marchers, and hard-chargin' grunts.
So your stubbed-toe warnings give us major **affront**.

C
If A Camel Is **Cranky**, What Does That Mean?

A camel who's **cranky** wants plenty of space.
Stand away from his mouth, or he'll spit in your face.

Cranky (CRANG-kee) *Adjective* — Having a bad disposition; peevish; irascible; discontented

A camel who's **cranky** feels most out of sorts,
Forget about spittle – he could bite off your shorts.

If A Dachshund Has A **Doppleganger**, What Does That Mean?

If a dachshund sees its **doppleganger**, he's found an unknown "twin."
If you meet your doppleganger, you'll swear they're mirrored kin.

Doppleganger (DAW-pull-gang-er) *Noun* – The unrelated look-alike of a living person or animal. **Dachshund** (DOX-hoont)

If the **dopplegangered** dachshunds chased a bunny just for fun,
That's a picture you could label: "Two hot dogs and a bun."

If A Gargoyle's **Grotesque**, What Does That Mean?

Gargoyles are statues, keeping watch from their roofs.
To say they are "ugly," is stating the truth.

Grotesque (gro-TESK) *Noun* — Outlandish or bizarre looking; marked by a distorted appearance; decorative art style employing usually ugly human or animal forms

But sometimes the truth can more kindly be said.
So let's just say gargoyles are... **grotesque** instead.

27

If A T-Rex Is **Testy**, What Does That Mean?

If a T-Rex is **testy**, he's mean and he's prickly.
Would spiffy new shoes help cheer him up quickly?

TESTY (TESS–tee) *Adjective* – Irritated, huffy, cross, ornery, disagreeable

Oh, wait – we forgot – he'll still feel **testy**,
He can't reach the laces from his short-armed chesty.

O
If Otters Love To **Osculate**, What Does That Mean?

If otters share a webbed-foot hug, and then a whiskered nuzzle,
They're likely soon to **osculate**, muzzle kissing muzzle.

Osculate (OS-cu-late) *verb* – 1. A kiss; kissing; 2. (mathematics) when one curve or surface touches another curve or surface.

Some **osculators** pucker well – others slip, or lack much heft.
But you otter not steal a kiss; that's **osculation** theft.

31

C If A Cobra Is **Colubrine**, What Does That Mean?

If something is dog-like, it's "canine," while "feline" means just-like-a-cat.
Cow-like's "bovine" (a term so divine), and "murine" means just-like-a-rat.

Colubrine (KOL-you-brine) *Noun* – Of, or relating to, or resembling a snake

But the phrase that dazzles King Cobra – he thinks it's hissingly fine –
Which means "like a snake," is Scrabble-word great,
is that serpentine word, **colubrine**.

If A Monkey Is **Malodorous**, What Does That Mean?

If a monkey is **malodorous**, that's worse than plain P.U.
Think rank and skunky, funky monkey – topped with baby poo.

Malodorous (mahl-OH-der-us) *Noun* — Stinky; foul smelling; putrid; rank

Worse yet, that swingin' primate brags, "My life is such a gas."
No need to say, "How right you are!" just keep breathing through your mask.

If A Jackrabbit's Got **Jactitations**, What Does That Mean?

If a rabbit out Montana way, exhibits **jactitations**,
That means he twitches, twirls and jumps – full body palpitations.

Jactitations (jak-tih-TAY-shuns) *Noun* — Involuntary spasm of a muscle or limb; body twitching

Of course, his explanation differs. (Is it me, or was he smirking?)
What we call **jactitations** he calls, "wild-rabbit twerking."

A Quail's Quiescent Confection – What Does That Mean?

Whilst off for a sail, a **quiescent** quail, prefers both peace and quiet.
No sudden sneeze, no cannons please, and surely no seagull riot.

Quiescent (Kwy–ES-cent) *Adjective* — Calm, inactive, quiet; no motion; causing no trouble or symptoms.

In fact, the calming item that, the quail calls "near perfection,"
Is a popsicle break, each night quite late – a **quiescently**-frozen confection.

Acknowledgments

The following individuals were responsible, in myriad ways, for the creation and completion of this book. Space limitations prohibit me from including details, but I trust each of them knows how their respective time, ideas or assistance helped make this book possible. I'm genuinely thankful to each of them. *Rocket Roddy*

Maureen Sanford
Thelma & Earl Beck
E. F. Cudignotto
Phil, Leslie, Amanda & Tess Stewart
Mily Erister Camejo
Bev Questad
Hugh Murray

Kellee, Jake & Wyatt Gibbons
Lisa Pennington
Anita West
Mirla Dosantos Cruz
Debora Emmert
Don Margraf
Paula Zellner

Lynn & Michelle Jennings
C. Perez-Giraldez
Mary Bahrami
April, Praise, Naira & Harry, of littlelabradoodle.com
Ricardo Ruelos

THANK YOU!

Thank you for reading our book!
If you loved it, please consider leaving a review.

SOME FREEBIES FOR YOU!

Visit us at www.rocketroddyauthor.com
to get additional resources and freebies.
We will also keep you up to date with new offerings and updates.

www.rocketroddyauthor.com